Search Engine Optimization 2017

The Complete Step-by-Step Guide to Search engine optimization for Beginners

Table of Contents

Introduction

Congratulations on downloading your personal copy of *Search Engine Optimization 2017.* Thank you for doing so.

The following chapters will discuss some of the many ways that you can optimize your website to get the best search engine rankings.

You will discover how important it is to have substantial content.

The final chapter will explore the best way to make sure that your website gets the most exposure possible.

There are plenty of books on this subject on the market, thanks again for choosing this one! Every effort was made to ensure it is full of as much useful information as possible. Please enjoy!

Congratulations on downloading your personal copy of the *name of the book.* Thank you for doing so.

Chapter 1: Ways that Google Works

Google can sometimes be difficult to figure out. This is especially true with all of the new software that is available for search engines, and for those who want to be able to beat the algorithms that are set up with search engines, it is important that you work to make sure that you are figuring out the right way to do things, and that you are getting the most out of the Google experience.

It is also important to know that you are getting the right information. There are a lot of people who simply don't know what they are talking about and they will pass this information onto others – they either do it because they *think* they know what they are doing and want to pass it along or they do it on purpose with the intention of not letting anyone in on their secret. You want to make sure that you are doing it the right way so that you draw more traffic, instead of ruining the traffic that you have and destroying your performance.

In the Past

Google's original intention was to draw people to sites that were relevant to what they were looking for. They wanted people to see the best sites, and they came up with algorithms that would later be commonly known as crawlers that are searching the web to be able to find everything that you want to know about each of the subjects that you put into that search bar.

These crawlers weren't foolproof, though. People learned quickly that they could scam the crawlers. If they wanted those who were looking for a keyword to find them, they would just stuff their sites with a keyword. For example:

If you had a website that you wanted people who were searching for "best dog collars" to visit, you would just need to put "best dog collars" a ton of times into your site. Then, when people typed that in, you would be the first one to come up. This was a problem, though, because Google wanted people to get the most relevant results and sometimes that would lead them to scamming sites.

This practice of keyword stuffing was quickly taken care of, and Google changed its allowances to only including sites that were between 1 and 2% of the keyword that people wanted on there.

As more people figured out how to "beat" the algorithms, Google responded by having different requirements for the sites to be able to make it onto the search engine list.

Google is constantly making updates that are changing the way that people can get led to sites. After abolishing keyword stuffing, they then had to focus on backlink stuffing, where sites had thousands of the same link that all led back to the same page to make the page seem more relevant. With every move that black hat search engine optimization "experts" made, Google had a counter move that allowed them the chance to make sure that they were going to be able to beat it.

This isn't to say, though, that those who practice white hat search engine optimization are able to make sure that they are getting the best experience possible from Google. People who make sure that they are doing things the right way should have no problem getting ranked. The point of it, though, is that they need to make sure that they are able to get the real idea of search engine optimization and the way that it works before they can begin to make sure that it is truly working for them. Here are the things that you will need to be able to get what you want out of Google ranking:

Trust – you need to have a trustworthy site. Have backlinks that go to legitimate other sites and content that is of high quality. The crawlers will notice.

Authority – you should be an expert or at least *look* like an expert. You should have a lot of social media followers that are reflected on your site, and you should also have a lot of information that is included on the site that is similar to the social media. You should be sharing things from your site on social media and making sure that the two are as connected as possible.

Relevance – not only do you need keywords, but you also need to make sure that they are put in your content in a way that makes sense

As long as you have these things on your site, you will be able to make sure that you are getting the best experience possible on your site

The easiest way to understand Google is that you need to have relevant keywords, but not too many. You need to have a lot of high-quality authority, and you need to be a site that is trustworthy and has been around for, at least, a year or so.

Chapter 2: The Balance of Keywords

One of the most important things that you will do when you are studying search engine optimization and learning the right way to put search engine optimization to work on your site is keyword research. This can be anything from finding what works for your site to getting the information that you need to know about each of the keywords that people are searching for right now about what your site has to offer.

You need to do keyword research because you need to have the right keywords so that the right people are led to your site – if you're selling fertilizer but people are looking for fertility help, and you use that as your keyword, there will be thousands of people who come to your site learning how to have a baby, and you'll just be selling them bags of minerals and animal dung. You will have wasted all the effort that you put into search engine optimization just to get the wrong people to your site.

You also need to make sure that you are doing the right type of keyword search for the rankings that you want. This means that you will need to be sure that you are not trying to get too high of a ranking, especially at the beginning, because it will be too much of a goal to try to achieve if you are not prepared for that. Even the best sites may not have the best results when it comes to keywords.

We're getting ahead of ourselves, though.

Defining a Keyword

A keyword is something that you will use for your site to define your rank in the results. This can be anything from a single world – which is the traditional definition of a keyword to a long tail keyword that has several different words in it that make up a phrase. You may be better off with long tail, because it can be hard to rank (especially at the beginning) with single ones.

When you are getting started, long tail keywords will be your friend – they are easy to find, easy to do and easy to get the information for. They will also be able to help you figure out what you are doing and what is going to go on your site. The chances of ranking with a long tail keyword are much higher than ranking with a single one because of how competitive the other types are.

But, what are *Your* Keywords?

Every person who has every type of site and every reason for people to have to visit the site will have different keywords. The first step to finding your keywords is to make sure that you know what the keywords *could* be, so that you will be able to start the search for the other types of keywords.

Your keywords need to be relevant. While they are long-tailed, they also need to have a relatively narrow target to them that will allow you to zone in on what you want people to visit your site for a reason. You should be specific about things. If you sell children's pajamas, you could use things like:

Buy kids pajamas

Buy kids pajamas online

Online kids pajamas

Kids pajamas for sale

These are all things that people might type in a search engine when they are looking for pajamas for their children. They will not type in something like "picture of pajamas" or "DIY pajamas" because that is not what they are looking for, so try to avoid these (even if you *did* DIY these jammies)!

The Actual Keywords

If you're still lost on the keywords that you want to put on your site (which, we don't blame you – keywords are confusing), there are some things that you can do.

Steal them – the chances are that you have competitors even if you didn't know about it. Steal their keywords. As long as you don't steal their *content* (which is plagiarism, by the way), you will be just fine stealing their keywords. It is especially important to steal the ones from the competitors who are at the top of the rankings. It won't pay to steal the keywords from the ones who are on page eight of Google; because the chances are that their keywords aren't great.

Make your own list – if you know some of the things that you want your people to visit your site for, you can start to make a list. The easiest way to do this is to create three different columns of things. Try to use a spreadsheet program like Excel for this. You can put words in that at the beginning (like buy, purchase, where to get, get) then put the middle words (pajamas, kid's pajamas, jammies for kids, sleep pants, sleep shirts, kids PJS). Then, put the last part into it (online, high quality, custom made, cheap, cute, unique, new, USA). Add to these lists as many things that you can think of. Then, when you have about 5, at the *least,* in each of the lists, put them together in various combinations. If you have three lists (the beginning, middle, and end) with five in each of the lists, right there you will have 15 keywords that you can use. This will be long tail keywords. There will actually be more than that, but it is an easy minimum number to start with.

Will Your Keywords Work?

The only way that you can find out if they will work is to check with Google. Google has options with Ad Words that allow you to have a free account. From there, you can use the tools that are made for keyword planning. You can also get the "search volume and trends" button. Put your keywords into the area and then click the go button. It will allow you to see how many times the keyword got a search on Google. You should make sure that your keywords are used often and eliminate any one that has zero hits.

Chapter 3: The Actual Search Engine Optimization

Since you are not a web developer or a mastermind at managing the web page, the chances are that you cannot trick the search engine. That's not a good idea anyway, because Google has a huge team of specialists who are constantly trying to fight these guys and the chances are that you will not be able to use that trick for very long anyway. Instead, you should be trying to be legitimate about what you are offering on your site and the search engine options that you are putting into your site, so that Google will be able to pick up everything that you have on your site.

This is where you go to make sure that Google can see you. Your site should be optimized in the best way possible to make sure that you are getting the content visible, your site allows search engines to find it, and your keywords are making their appearance in the search engines so that your site will be visible.

Your URL

This is the first place that the search engines are going to find you. If you want people to visit a page on your site, you need to make sure that the URL is clean and that it has some of the keywords in the name of it. For example, if you are using the kid's pajamas.

Your site might automatically default to look like this: www.fakesite.com/page3/12812591?xxpage1/artic le4551

This is messy, and it is not something that you will be able to have shown up in search engines. You should make sure that you are changing your URLS so that they look neat and clean, you can do this through your website manager, but your URL should look something like this:

www.fakesite.com/kidspajamas/girlspajamas/

This is something that will change the way that your site looks, and it will be better than trying to make sure that you are getting what you want. The results will be more likely to show up on Google, and your visitors will know exactly where they are at when they look at your site.

The Backend

The site can be set up any way that you want it to be, so that you will be able to get the best results possible. Some people can make it in the way that they want, and some people choose to do it so that they can have the best search engine results – those who choose the second are the ones who have the most traffic to their site and can make sure that they are getting exactly what they need from the different options. It is a good idea to make it as easy as possible.

While some sites choose to put videos and images onto their site and then use anchor text to draw the search engines to them, there are others that simply use text on the pages that they want.

This is the best possible approach for you to use. When you have text on your site, you will be able to show the search engines what it is all about, and what is going on with your site, so that you don't have to worry about trying to get the anchor text right. Google will always pick up sites more that have text that is on the actual site instead of text that is just in the form of anchor text.

Too Much or Too Little

There are some people who have started preaching not to put any keywords into a page because of the threats that come from Google on their overstuffed pages policies, but that is going to be harmful to your site – Google can't find you without, at least, a few keywords.

In general, your keyword usage should be far under 2%. It should fall somewhere between 5% and 1%, but if it goes slightly over, the Google police will not come after you, and you will still be able to show up. The easiest way to do this is to design your site around a couple of keywords. This will allow you to write naturally around them and have the content that is in them. Alternatively, you can put a keyword here and there into the site to make sure that you are getting what you need. To ensure that you have the keywords weaved naturally in; always put them in the meta tags in the headings and sometimes in the content. You will also want them in the anchor text if you are using images or videos.

You can use a site like Ubersuggest and simply copy and paste your content into it to find out what your keyword percentage is. If it is too high, just get rid of a few of the keyword instances that are within the content.

Meta Tags

We mentioned Meta tags in the last little section, and it is entirely possible that you froze up with that mention. New webmasters, especially those who have very little experience with Google and search engine rankings, will sometimes be confused at the use of Meta tags. In the simplest form possible, these are what Google displays from your site. You can design your own or let Google take care of it for you. When you design your own, you can put your keywords into it and allow yourself to be able to make sure that you are getting many more hits on your site. If you do the tags the right way, you will get more traffic. The sites that allow you to create your own site – like WordPress and Wix – will enable you to put your Meta tags in. Simply look for the title information that is listed on your page in your back-office part of the website. If you use a website administrator, simply ask them if they can put the Meta tags in for you and you will have them showing up in your Google results in no time.

Chapter 4: Links Matter, Too

While your keywords are important, having links on your site is nearly as important if you want to make sure that you are going to be able to get the rankings that you want. You need to have the right links on your page to show Google that you are connecting with real sites and legitimate authorities. Google knows what you are linking to, and you need to make sure that you are prepared to show Google what you can do and who you are linking that is related to your site.

Different Links

There are many different options when it comes to putting links on your site. The only thing that is completely true all of the time, is that you use a link that will allow you to be able to link to something that is legitimate. For example, you don't want to link to a site that has a couple of posts and a whole bunch of ads. You don't want to link to something that you have only seen once or twice, and you seriously don't want to link to a scam site.

There is a lot of debate between which type of site that is the best to link to, but there is no real right or wrong in this case. Whether you are linking to an online store, a government site or a high authority blog, you will be able to enjoy the benefits that come with back linking and the information that is contained when you do the links as long as you are trying to make sure that you get all of that put into your site.

Getting Links

The easiest way to get links is to find them on your own. Find sites that you like, blogs that are informative and government information that backs up what you are talking about. Don't link to hundreds of different things all at once or Google will kick you off of any of their rankings, because that is a way to try and scam the system that was designed by Google. It is a good idea just to add links as you think of them and even design your blog posts around the links so that you can make sure that the links that you are using are the ones that are best for your site. It is always wise to find links on your own.

Don't pay for links. Don't ask people to buy your links to your site and certainly don't buy links to other sites. The links are all accessible and all free on the Internet, so just copy the links. Seriously, don't buy links. If Google finds out (and the chances are that they will), you will not be able to show up in the rankings at all. Google has policies that are in place and (even if you didn't read before agreeing) you are subject to those policies. Buying links go right along with that.

Don't Do It

Even if you find a trading link group, don't do that either. It is much easier (even if it does take longer) to try and build up the links on your site naturally so that you can have a legitimate site. There is no point in building it up fast because Google has an algorithm to figure out how fast you got those links and how much it made a difference to the way that you brought your site up. You will not show up in the results if you have not been allowed to grow your page links naturally. Trading is also against policy, although it is not specifically outlined. Avoid it.

Do not pay for a network to build your links. Even though it can help you to get what you want and they may seem legitimate when you are starting out, they are scammy and spammy. They will blast your site on message boards (don't do this either, it is in bad taste). You will build your links too quickly, Google will notice, and you'll be back at zero, so you'll have to start all over again.

The Anchors

The links that you have on your site will need to have anchors to them. In general, you need to make sure that your anchor text has the information that you need to make it better optimized for your site. For example, if you are linking to a site that has information about the best materials for your kid's pajamas, you should put materials for kid's pajamas on the anchor text, because it will have part of your keyword, and it will appear natural because you are not trying to stuff the whole keyword or all of your keywords into it.

Anchor text, by the way, is what you see when you look at a link. It is the clickable group of words (or single word) that you will be able to use to get to the link that the site has set up. This will allow you to make sure that you are getting what you need out of the anchors and the links. Your links will just look messy if you use the URL instead of anchor text, so get used to using the anchor text every time that you do a link ... even if it is just to an image.

Chapter 5: Getting Social on Your Site

Social media is important for checking up on your high school crush, and finding out when your nephew's birthday party is, but it is also really important if you want to make sure that you are using the site for the best experience. There are so many options that you have with social media that will allow you to make sure that you are getting what you need out of the experience and that you are going to be able to add the different options to your site.

The point is that if you want to rank higher in the search engines, you should take advantage of social media.

Social media is used to gain traffic to your site. You need to have a social media account of some sort if you want to get the most amount of traffic and if you want to ensure that you are going to be able to get everything that you want on your site. There are many different options that you can choose from when it comes to personal social media, but when you have a business, it can be hard to manage a website as well as three or four social media accounts. Instead, focus on one. When you feel confident with one of them, you can then move onto two.

Google Plus

The chances are that you don't use Google Plus for all of your social media needs. While the company is a technology giant, their social media platform just hasn't taken off like the company had hoped that it would. The majority of people who use +, use it for business purposes and make sure that they are using it when they are trying to get higher up in the rankings for their site on Google. The company has released various statements that show they do not take this into consideration, but there is proof that having a Google Plus account will help to increase your rankings on Google.

Businesses and search engine optimization experts all agree that Google *does* take it into consideration even if it is not something that they do on an official basis.

There is a good chance, though, that your competitors aren't using Google Plus, because it is not quite as popular. This means that you should be using it since they don't have the advantage of that when they are doing different things with their site. Google will not rank them as high as what it is ranking you, so you should make sure that you are using it in the best way possible.

Get a Google Plus account for your business (it's free!) and make sure that you add a follow button on your site.

Facebook

As the most popular social network in the world, Facebook just keeps growing and growing. What was once a simple site for Harvard students to connect with each other has grown by leaps and bounds in the years that it has been in business. Everyone uses Facebook and businesses are always making sure that they are on there and that they are relevant when it comes to the different things that are going on with the site. You should make sure that your business is working to be on Facebook and that it has *all* of the information you want.

The easiest way to make your Facebook relevant is to update it often. It is a good idea to post something about once a day. Post a link to something that is on your site every other day and be sure that you share lots of information and pictures. Like things that are from other businesses related to yours and keep the pictures updated about your business so that it has a lot of activity.

Always make sure that you have your website address listed on your Facebook and that it is clickable. Everything that you post should have a link back to your site, so that people can easily visit you.

When you are sure that your Facebook is ready to go and that you have designed it in the correct way, you will need to make sure that you are putting a "like" button on your website. This will allow people to go to your Facebook. When they like you, they will start to see your content and everything that you share (with your links) and they will then be led back to your site.

If you have both a Facebook and a Google Plus account, you will have a higher chance of getting more followers, and this will enable you to get the most amount of traffic possible. One of the great things about having both is that you will be able to post the same things to both of them. For example, you can use an app like IFTTT which stands for "if this, then that." You can set it up so that if you post to Facebook, then you will also post the same thing to Google Plus. You can even use this for several different sites that will allow you to easily manage many different social media sites at once – this is the only way that you will be able to do it without having to hire a social media manager or someone who can work specifically on that.

Your search engine optimization on social media matters, too. Make sure that you are using your keywords and that you are always back linking to your site. There are many different things that you can put on social media, so make sure that you are using search engine optimization. Even Facebook uses keywords to help people find you. One thing that you *don't* want to do in the beginning is pay for Facebook advertising. Instead, use that money to help make your actual site better and get people drawn into that first.

Chapter 6: Measuring Success with Analytics

All of this will be for naught if you do not know how successful you are with the sites that you are using and the keywords that you have put onto your site and your social media. You need to keep track of how it is going and what you are doing, so that you can make sure that you are as successful as possible. It is wise to make sure that you are doing well and always to check the progress that you have made so that you will not have to worry about the problems that come along with all of the options that are on your site.

Analytics will tell you what your traffic is, how much you have had come to your site and what it looks like to other people.

Google Analytics

This is the most common platform that people choose to use when they are looking at the different traffic things that are going on with their businesses. This is probably because most people are only worried about their Google rankings and some of the other search engines are simply not on their radar. Google makes it easy to see where you stand and to see how many people are coming to the site directly from Google. It is easy to compare what you are doing to what you *need* to be doing when you know the analytical aspect of the process.

Google Analytics will allow you to see how much traffic you have, what is going on with your site and what you need to do. It is free for Google users.

All you need to do is create an account if you don't have one or use the account that you already have on Google. If you go to google.com/analytics you can see everything that you need to know about your site once you have signed up for the analytics account.

Using It

You can use the data that you get from Google to see how your site is doing and what you can improve on.

Comparison feature – Analytics allows you to compare two completely different times and dates to see what was going on with your site then. As long as you have the right URL in there, Google can see how many people came to your site, how long they stayed for and whether they clicked onto different pages within the site. It is a great way to see if people are staying and what you need to do to make sure that you are doing the right things.

The easiest comparison that you can make is a date, when you first started your site to today's date. Look at the differences in the dates and then be sure that you are going to be able to get the most out of the sites and that people are visiting it. If you don't have a lot of visitors or if there is no change between then and now, you have a problem.

Charts – you can see the charts over a period, too. You don't have to just look at the two different dates that you originally compared and, instead, you will be able to figure out what is going on with your site over a period. This is great if it seems like you are having a lot of traffic and then no traffic at all. You can see the trends and then predict what is going to happen with those trends each time that you do something different on your site. As long as you are looking at the right URL, this information is accurate, and you can see if things like the season or even the time of day are affecting your traffic.

Where it Comes From

To figure out what you need to be targeting and the things that you need to do to make sure that you are getting traffic, you need to know where your traffic is coming from. You can use Google Analytics to help yourself find this so that you will be able to get the most out of the data that you have. If you want to be able to find the best information on analytics, you will need to find the acquisition section that shows you what is going on with the site and where your traffic is coming from. If it is coming from Facebook, bulk up the posts that you do on there. If it is coming from Google, add some different ads that are related to your site on there. You can choose where you are going to do paid advertising when you know what it is. Up until this point, you should not be doing any paid ads because you don't know where the right traffic is or what the right place to advertise would be.

Organics

There are many people who probably come from your site right from the search engine. These are organic clicks to the site and organic visits. Google makes sure that it has that information written down and that you can learn what you need to make sure that you are targeting the right keywords and the right people. By using the organic search information that you can find on

Analytics, you can see how well your keywords are doing and what you need to do to make sure that you are going to be able to get the most out of the search engines that you are using. It is wise to make sure that you use this to your advantage and that you are going to get the most out of it when it comes to the searches that you can do on your site.

Always use the information that you find on analytics. It is a great free tool that will not only help you to improve your site but will also help you to find out what you can be doing better. It is a great tool and something that no other search engines have – Google has made it easier to figure out *how* you can improve your search engine and your rankings.

Chapter 7: Problems with Search Engine Optimization

Now that we are quickly approaching the halfway mark of this book with all of the information that you need to know about search engine optimization and figuring out how to get your site to rank, it is a good idea to mention that there can be some problems with search engine optimization. The chances are that you already knew that, but by looking at the problems in a deeper way, you will be better prepared for them and to overcome them (or avoid them altogether).

No Listing

There is a chance that your site won't even show up on Google. That means that you are not listed, and you will not be able to make sure that you are getting the information that you need. People aren't able to find you, and you will not be able to show up when there are search engines for your keywords. Always be sure that you are doing what you can and that you are getting the best experience by showing up on Google.

Your site is probably not listed because it is new, it hasn't been shared on social media, or it does not have any content on it.

If you want to see whether you are just not showing up in the results or you are not showing up altogether, put "site:yoursitename.com" in the Google search bar. If you see any results, you are on Google but just not getting the results that you want.

No Ranking

When someone puts in a good keyword, they *could* go to your site if it is optimized. When someone puts in your site name, they *should* go to your site. Sometimes, though, you might not even rank for the name of your business. This usually only happens with sites that are brand new, so you need to let them know that you are on there.

Just link to your site. This should be done with the links on your anchor text. You can also add some other ones and then Google will be able to see that your site exists. Have some patience as it can take a while for you to be listed.

Another way that you can do this is to list your business on yellow pages, white pages, and Yelp. This is a business listing, and it will allow you to see that you are doing it. Always link to your site when you are filling this information out. Try to find at least 50 different places where you can list your site so that you can make sure that you come up. It will work most of the time. As long as you have social media and some other links (around 50 will do the trick), you should start to see your business come up when you type in the name of your business.

Dropping Rankings

Once your site is ranking, you may think that the work is done. It is not, though. You need to make sure that you are always doing the work to get yourself ranking. If you don't, your site will begin to drop off and will not show up in all of the rankings that are available. Things that you can do to make sure that you are always able to stay on top:

- Link on social media
- Backlink to other sites
- Get your name out there
- Try some campaigns (cheap!) with ads
- Let people know that your site is out there
- Stay relevant with content – keyword rich blog posts are wonderful for this

Penalties

The chances are that, if Google is penalizing you, you are doing something that could be considered a black hat or unethical. If it happens that there is some update that is going to penalize you for what you are doing, you will have to change what you are doing and make sure that you are going to get the most out of the process. It also means that you will need to make sure that people can see your site and that you are doing everything that you can.

Try to change the things that you are doing – remember that you want to be a legitimate site, not something that is spammy or scammy for people to visit. It is important that you follow each of these things and that you always do things according to Google's policies.

If you find that you are being penalized, rewrite your site and the search engine optimization that you have on it. It will be easy to do because you'll have the framework – just make sure that you do it legitimately this time.

Building Up Your Search Engine Optimization

There is a chance that your search engine optimization may not be ranking or may not be what you want it to be even after following each of the principles that are outlined in this book. While it is always a good idea to try things on your own, sometimes that just doesn't work, and you will have to find professional help. The best part about this is that you don't always have to pay to have a search engine optimization expert.

There are plenty of real experts that are online. As long as you stay away from search engine optimization blogs and people who tout their "perfect" methods, you can find everything that you need to know about search engine optimization on the Internet. This can be anything from the help that Google provides to Word Press and everything in between. The Wix application is designed to make your site easily optimized, so try to use that to your advantage. They even have a wizard that you can follow to make sure that your site is getting the most hits and that your keywords are where they need to be –take advantage of this, because it comes along with the site that you have.

Chapter 8: The Original Search Engine Optimization – Local

The chances are that you know what businesses are, and where they are located in your town because of the local search engine optimization that is used by Google to direct people to pages based on their location and the way that they are going to be able to use them. Google has created options that allow you to make sure that you are getting the things that you need from your search engines. If you have a true brick and mortar business, you should be utilizing local search engine optimization to lead people to your site so that they can find you based on their location. It is great for people who want others who are close to them to be able to find them.

The way that people search for your business in a local sense is different from organic search engine terms in that they can find you on a map. They will see your information (often with a clickable phone number), the hours that you are open and information on the quality of your business based on the reviews that other people have left about it on the same site. It is easy for people to find you, contact you and visit your website based on the local information that Google has on you.

Ranking

Just like the traditional search engine optimization and the organic search engines that you are going to be able to show up on, you will need to make some effort to be able to be seen on the search engine. This means that you will need to try to rank. There is a different course that you can take to find the way that you are going to be able to get local search results and you must make sure that you are getting what you can out of each of these when you are working your business. You should have all of this information on your site so that Google will put you up as a truly listed business:

- Address
- Google My Business information
- Location of your address
- Domain name and authority
- HTML Name
- Consistency of the site
- Legitimacy of your site and business
- Keywords that are in a title
- Business listing name
- Rates that are achieved from your rankings

If you want to be able to show up on the local rankings for Google, you need to have these things as a minimum.

For example, if you are going to have your site listed as a physical site but someone else has something similar in the same area as you, you will need to work harder to make sure that you show up first. The chances of this happening in a big city are very high – you will almost always need to utilize search engine optimization to be sure that you are going to show up first in the rankings. In a small town with not so many small businesses (especially if you have a specific niche), you will not have to worry about the specific competition as much as when you were doing each of the other things that are listed in that ranking.

Google My Business

This is a tool that many small businesses utilize and that you can take advantage of if you are going to be having a physical location for your business (or even if you already do). You need to make sure that you have everything that is required on the My Business page. You should make sure that you have the name of the business, the information that is required to contact you if something happens or if a customer simply wants to come to your business (these can be different numbers) and the way that you can rank according to the different sites. It is a good idea to fill this profile out completely. Always make sure that it links back to your site and that the site that is listed on your website is your homepage of the specific site that you want to be able to use.

Always choose a category that makes sense for your business. For example, if you are selling pajamas, you wouldn't want to make your category web services or anything other than clothing or retail.

Citations Are Important

Similar to how you had to list your business in directories to get your website name out there, you will need to do the same thing with your physical business and the directories that are available. In general, it is a good idea to make sure that you have around 50 different directories listing for your business. Always link all of the information for your business including your website, your phone number and any other contact information for your business. It is a good idea to try and make sure that it is listed as often as possible.

Reviews

This is another important part of the way that you can do things on your site and with your local listing. You will need to make sure that you have all of the information that you need on your site so that you will be able to get the listing done right. Having reviews will be able to help you figure out what you are going to have and will allow people to understand that you are a legitimate company.

Never pay for reviews!

The easiest way to get reviews is to ask people who have legitimately used your service for their review of the company. Have them visit your site and then have them go to Google to leave their review. It is very simple to do so if they have a Google account and it only takes a few minutes. People who are happy with your services will most likely be very willing to give you a good review. This is the only way that you will be able to get legitimate reviews that are ethical and do not go against any of the policies that are included with Google My Business.

Chapter 9: Using Schema and Micro data

There are many different sites that have information on them that people are not able to access because there is simply too much information. This is something similar to search engines but is also different in that you need to make sure that you are going to be able to show up in the different options that are included on sites.

These sites cause the search engines to crawl over them and find the information that you need to make sure that you are getting the most out of. Doing this is the easiest way for you to increase what you are doing.

It is exactly what some of the bloggers are talking about when they say that meta doesn't matter anymore. Instead, the things like micro data matter and allow people to be sure that they are going to get all of the information that they need.

Micro data is different than meta in that it allows search engines to find you more easily and gives you the chance to show off the different options that you have.

Schema

The schema is a site that you can find what you need to make sure that you have the best micro data possible. It is something that all of the search engines use, and it has all of the information that you will need to be able to get the best experience possible and have all of the data that you need to put into it. There are many different meta-data problems that can be solved by using Schema. There are many ways that you can use Schema to find out the best way to put your rankings at the top.

What to Have

Since Schema is recognized by Google and is the most common thing that you can use to make sure that you are getting the information that you need, it is something that will allow you the chance to do more with your data. You need to make sure that you are following all of the information that Schema has so that you will be able to get the best markup experience possible with your micro data. You need to have the best reviews, followers, and products. Micro data will also include mentions of your site name and the other information about your business that is included with content, videos, music and even with events that are listed in various formats, including with social media mentions. It is a good idea to try and figure this out by formatting the codes.

Always add a description, the address and your business name to your information so that the code is prioritized. The Schema approach would be to show that the site has a lot of information on it and that it has a phone number and even an address. By using Schema, you will help Google to pick up on the business listing. It will simply be like reminding the spiders to pick it up as they crawl through the various information. Try to make sure that you are adding all of the data that you need to your site before you write it out so that you don't have to go back and retag anything.

Facebook

Even though Google and Bing and even Yahoo accept the coding that is implemented by Schema, there is always something that will make things more difficult for webmasters. In this case, it is that Facebook does not recognize this. It is something that will make it harder for you if you are trying to get a social following (which you should be doing) and if you have a business that is close to your area, you need to make sure that you have it listed as such.

Similar to how having a social media profile will help you when it comes to traditional search engines, it will also help you when it comes to local search engine optimization. You need to make sure that you are using the Open Graph Language that Facebook recognizes so that you can be sure that you are going to make sure that you can have your business listed on Facebook. People will also be able to follow you more easily if they have everything that they need to know right there in front of them.

Use the Open Graph tool to add everything that you want to your Facebook. The main things that you should have are all of the types of your contact information. You should have the phone number to your business as well as the website where people can find you. This will allow you to see that you can do different things with your Facebook and that you can add all of the contact information that you need.

There are many people who do not have local search engine optimization because they do not think that they need it. These are mostly online businesses that do not plan to open a brick and mortar location because they do the majority of their business online, but you should still have the local search engine optimization because it will allow you to have a better chance at people

SEARCH ENGINE OPTIMIZATION 2017

coming to your site.

One thing that you can do if you want to make sure that people don't just show up at the office where you work, is to make sure that you are only going to be able to be open at certain times. When you set up your Google profile and the information for your business, make sure that you put in that you are only available by appointment and that people cannot visit your business unless they have gone to your website or talked to you on the phone first. This will keep the majority of unwanted visitors away while still allowing you to have that important local listing on Google that will help to increase the traffic that you get on your site.

Chapter 10: Tools You Need For Search Engine Optimization

Search engine optimization isn't just all about what you can do on your own. While it is beneficial to be able to do the majority of things that are on search engine optimization on your own and you can help yourself by not having to hire a professional, you will still need to use some tools.

There is no way around using the tools – they are designed for everyone who wants to do search engine optimization from the people who are professionals to novices who are just getting started with search engine optimization. This means that you will need to make sure that you are getting everything that you want and that you are going to be able to put up the information that you want on your site. There is no way to get a lot of traffic unless you use the tools that are given to you. While the majority of basic tools that you need for simply search engine optimization are free, there are some that do cost money, and you will need to figure out how to use these and what the best approach is when you are considering all of the costs of your business and your website.

AdWords Planner – you need to make sure that you are getting the right keywords. Google AdWords Planner is the best thing to being able to do this. You can find out the number of times that a keyword can be used and a number of times that you need to make sure that it is used. There are many different options that you can select when you are using this tool, so make sure that you choose the one that is going to work the best for you. It is best to make sure that you know what type of traffic you want to be able to get before you use planner.

Trends – see how you can figure out the market that you have. It will allow you to adjust your information so that you can get the best rankings. When you use Trends, you will be able to find out what you need to do to figure out the way that you are doing different things and how you can control the different options that are listed in your search engine optimization ranking. It will also give you an idea to compare yourself to competitors, to your past site and the market overall.

Samurai – you can use this to help yourself figure out the basics of your keywords. It is different than AdWords in that it gives you ideas based on your site and the market that you are a part of instead of being based on different keywords that you have put into it. It will allow you the chance to make sure that you are getting the best keywords and that you will be able to add all of the different information to it. There are many different options, and this has a free version as well as a paid version that allows you to do so much more.

Moz – the search engine optimization experts. You can find everything that you need to know about your site, the way that it ranks, your keyword and even your brand. You will even be able to get suggestions that are right on your site, and you can see how the crawlers are going to work on your site. There are, again, two version of this. The paid version of Moz offers a lot more, and you can even get some free search engine optimization classes from the site. It allows you to become certified in search engine optimization so that if you get really good at it, you can offer search engine optimization to other people and make money that way.

Analyzer – this is different than the other tools in that it looks at your site and it can see the different ways that the keywords are going to work on your site. There are many different options that you can find on here, and you will be able to see which keywords are working and which are not. Use the ones that work the best and eliminate the other ones to replace them with keywords that are going to be the best. This is especially helpful if you already have a site and just need to upgrade the search engine optimization on it to make sure that you will be able to add the different things.

Search engine optimizationQuake – you can use this to see where you stand on Google. It is easy to see it from Google, but you will sometimes have trouble finding that when you need it, so make sure that you are finding the best options for yourself. There are many different ways to use Quake, so be sure that you try all of the options. While you can purchase upgrades, you can get everything that you need from the free words that are listed on there.

Ubersuggest – one of the best keyword mention sites. It will show you the long tail keywords that you need. These are all based on data that is gathered from crawlers, and it will tell you that you need to make sure that you are getting the best information possible. You will also need to figure out the right way to be able to get the information downloaded. When you find these keywords, add them to your site and make sure that they are all in there in the right way – don't overstuff them. This site is also great because it allows you to see if you are using too many keywords. You can just copy and paste your content for the exact percentage of the keywords that you have. If you are over 2%, you need to rethink the keywords and try something else that will allow you to not have too many. The crawlers will not like it if you have too many keywords because it will look like you are trying to stuff it full. Use this to determine that and figure out if you have too many or too few.

Chapter 11: The Updates on Google

There is always a chance that Google will change the way that they do things. In fact, it is very likely that it is going to happen and it is something that you will need to handle when it does happen. You should always do your best to be prepared if Google decides to change the way their algorithm works. It is a good idea to have a site that is functional and one that is ready to be updated at any time ifGoogle updates their rules.

As long as you are making sure that you are using white hat techniques (like the ones that are included in this book) to optimize your site, you will not need to worry about getting dropped as a result of the changes that Google is trying to make. It is a good idea to try and be sure that you are putting everything on your site so that you can make changes to it.

HTTPS

One of the most recent updates that Google did to the way that they rank things, allows HTTPS sites to always come before sites that are simply HTTP.

Leading up to this, there were many sites that were simply not secure. People did not understand that because they simply figured that a site was a site – it was hard to tell a difference between HTTP and HTTPS for people who were making sure that things were working out the right way. When someone wanted to visit a site, they were at risk if it was not HTTPS.

While Google will still accept sites that are only HTTP and not have the secure S at the end of them, it will always rank the sites that have HTTPS higher than the ones that do not. This is not a problem if you do not have a lot of competitors or anyone who is trying to rank higher than you, but it does become a problem when you realize that it is nearly impossible to rank above the HTTPS if you only have an HTTP site. It isn't about the fact that your site isn't secure – it is simply done because your site might *not* be secure instead of being totally secure like the HTTPS. Encryption is simple to do and just a small change that you can make. If you are using a program for your site, just change your encryption to secure so that you can make sure that you are always above the HTTP sites.

Blocking Doors

A doorway page is a page that does just that – creates a doorway that leads people to a different area. It means that you must make sure that you are going through the different things and that you are going to be able to get to the site only if you go through the doorway.

The site is usually one that is intended *just* for optimization purposes. If you have ever been to a site that tells you to "click here" to go to the "actual site" you have been to a doorway site. It is important to note that you will need to make sure that you are not using a doorway site.

Google recently made changes that allowed for the ranking to knock down doorway pages. While you can still have one and you can still rank, you will not be able to rank as high as what you once were with doorway pages. Google has done this to make sure that they are not being used for their search engine optimization efforts and that you are going to be able to include all of the different things with your site.

On Mobile

There are many instances where you will not be able to see a site on a mobile device simply because you are using a mobile device. This is because the site is not optimized for mobile viewing. Not only will you need to make sure that your site can be seen on a mobile device, but you should also make sure that you are using the mobile search engine optimization techniques that are included with the different things.

Google will always rank pages higher when they can be seen on mobile and when they are also able to be done on a mobile device. You need to make sure that you are prepared for the things that come along with mobile rankings, and it is a good idea to try and make sure that you are getting each of the different things that you want with your mobile devices. There are so many options that are included with mobile viewing, so be sure that you have done the best job possible to be able to include mobile devices.

While you may not necessarily get more traffic on a mobile device than you would get on a typical desktop site (which, you may get more traffic from mobile), you will be able to show up higher in the rankings if you are prepared with a mobile device. There are many different benefits that come with mobile devices, so just be sure that you are using them to your advantage – in a world where nearly everyone carries a smartphone, tablet or both, your site should be prepared for people to view it on that mobile device instead of on a bulk laptop or desktop computer that they need to lug around.

Chapter 12: AdWords and Spending Your Money

AdWords is not only a way for you to make sure that you are getting everything that you need from your site, but it is also a powerful advertisement tool that you can use to make sure that you are going to be able to get more views. The point of AdWords is that people can advertise their relevant products on the pages that there are search engines. Google allows businesses to purchase advertisements that other people will be able to see and it is a good idea to try and make sure that you are doing everything that you can to include the options that are listed on your AdWords.

When you want to do an ad on Google, you will need to use AdWords. This means that you will need to make an advertisement. The ad should be relevant to the keywords that people are going to search for when they want to see what you have.

For example, you can put an advertisement for unique, organic pajamas that shows only when people search for kid's pajamas. You can also connect it with other categories so that you can make sure that it is only showing up when you want it to, but make sure that you are doing what you can to be able to put different things on your site.

The way that AdWords works is that it is a pay per click model. If someone clicks on the ad that you have put on Google, you will have to pay for it. Until then, you do not pay to advertise. There are many different things that you can do to make sure that you have enough money to get the clicks that you want. AdWords will first ask you to set up a budget that you can use to be able to put your information in. This means that you will need to put things like your payment method, the information that will be used to contact you and then the ad that you want.

Your Ad

The ad that Google puts on the results will look almost identical to the other search engine results except for it will be at the very top of the page. It will be something that you can see when you do a search, and people will often think that it is part of the search. As long as the search is related to what you are doing, you will not have to worry about whether or not you are trying to fool your customers. Just be sure that you put in the information that you want and you will be able to have that ad listed.

The ad should have the information that you want people to know. It should be keyword optimized, but it should also be as natural as possible. Be sure that you have the right address for them to click on, the name that you want the ad to be and the information that you want people to see in the ad.

Spending

You can and should set up your spending for your ad before you make the decision to put the ad on Google. You will need to put payment information in, so make sure that you have a budget that you are going to set to be able to make sure that you are getting the most out of the ad. In general, you should expect to spend around $500 for the first ad. This is a low amount of advertising compared to traditional methods, so be sure that it is what you need to do.

When you set this up, you can have AdWords cut off at the amount that you want to spend. It will stop showing the ad when you have used up all of the funds that you set aside. At this point, Google will ask you if you want to renew it or if you want to add more money to it, so make sure that you are prepared for what you are going to spend in the future.

Additional Ads

You can then put additional ads on the site. Make sure that the site did well and that the ads worked out. Use the Google tools to be able to figure out if it increased your rankings and if it increased the amount of traffic that you can get to your site. If it does increase either of these things, you can make sure that you are going to get what you need out of it. This means that you should make another ad and put it on there. The chances are that it paid off more than what you were thinking and that you will be able to benefit from this process.

Don't Do It Yet

Don't jump into ads right away. You should first see if you can get traffic on your own. There are many different ways that you can get the traffic, so try it on your own (the freeway) first and then if that does not work, turn your attention to the ads that you can create with Google. If you are going to add different things to the ad, make sure that you keep track of them so that you can remember it later on when you *do* decide to do the ad at the right time.

Try Different Ones

There is a chance that the same people see your ad over and over again. It can be stale to them and may not make them want to click on it. To combat this, divide up your budget between two or more ads and then try to see if those are what will allow you the chance to be able to see that you are doing more. You should try to put new ads in all of the time and then see how each one performs. Tweak them until you are ready to make sure that they are all being done the right way.

Chapter 13: Looking at All Search Engine Optimization

After reading through each of the chapters, you should be able to have a good idea of what search engine optimization should mean to your site. It is a good idea to try different things with search engine optimization and make sure that you know what you are doing. The hope is that you read this *before* you create your site, so that you can apply each of these principles to your site. It is important that you do it before creating your site, so that you don't have to try to change the formatting of each of the different things on your site.

Designing the Site

One thing that you should remember is that your site design does not matter quite as much as your content on your site. Your visitors will appreciate a site that is designed nicely, but they will want to be able to get to the site first. Impress the crawlers with your content and then worry about impressing the people who came to the site from the search engine. You will have much better results.

Keywords are Important

While some blogs and other people like to preach that keywords don't matter anymore, they most definitely do. You need to have the right keywords to get the right results, and you will be able to see a huge increase in the traffic that comes to your site. If you are working to make sure that you are getting the most amount of traffic, you will be able to increase the number of rankings that you get on Google and even other search engines. Try your best when it comes to Google, and you will get the results that you need.

Make Money from Traffic

Once you have the traffic that you want, learn the right way to convert that. Just because you have a lot of people who are coming to your site doesn't mean that you are going to automatically make more money because of it. There are many different things that you need to do – including having something for sale on your site, but that is all dependent on the traffic that you get. No matter how great of a product you are selling, you won't be able to sell it if you don't have that required traffic.

Learning More

It is entirely possible to optimize your site without any further training, but you may need it if you plan to make your site the best possible. There are many different things that you can do with your site so make sure that you know what you are doing. It is a good idea to try to find out what you can do, how much you can work to make it happen and the right way to optimize your site. Keep in mind that you might need extra training if you want to be able to do your optimization in the best way possible.

Applying it All

Once you have learned everything that you can about optimization and the way that search engine optimization can help you with your website, you will be able to apply it to your site. If you see great results from it, you may consider different search engine optimization options. One thing that many people who are good at search engine optimization choose to do is either teach people or offer their optimization services to other websites so that they will be able to sell their services to people who want to get more from their sites – you can turn into the expert at search engine optimization.

Conclusion

Thanks for making it through to the end of *Search Engine Optimization 2017.* Let's hope it was informative and able to provide you with all of the tools you need to achieve your goals of making the most of your sites.

The next step is to make sure that you know the right way to optimize your site and to add that optimization to the site.

Finally, if you found this book useful in any way, a review on Amazon is always appreciated!

www.ingramcontent.com/pod-product-compliance
Lightning Source LLC
La Vergne TN
LVHW052311060326

832902LV00021B/3820